T0007104

Higher
Knowledge

Higher
Knowledge

SANAA's Rolex Learning Center
at EPFL Since 2010

Christophe Van Gerrewey

More than ten years have passed since the opening of the Rolex Learning Center at EPFL in 2010, and during this decade so much has happened that the world seems a different place. The density of events and changes in such a short time span is ostensibly unprecedented; if future historians want to characterize this period, they may be tempted to summarize it as an era of continuous disruption, in which the most unlikely and surprising things succeeded each other at breakneck speed.

It has become clear, for example, that for the first time in its history, mankind has to face the fact that it has severely, and probably irreversibly, damaged the planet on which it has been living. Not only has this been proved by statistics and science, but it has also become physically perceptible: the 2010s were the hottest decade in recorded history, with 2016 the hottest year and 2019 the second hottest ever, although global carbon emissions have not exactly declined inversely—on the contrary. The worldwide financial crisis that started around

2008 continues to have an increasing impact on the daily lives of billions of people: in most cases, it simply means that we all have to work more than before. In the second decade of the twenty-first century, terrorist incidents occurred almost everywhere, organized by individuals or movements of all tendencies. Revolts and revolutions in the Arabic world and a civil war in Syria caused a refugee crisis beginning in 2015, with thousands of people crossing the Mediterranean Sea at the peril of their lives. In 2016, a small majority of British citizens voted in favor of leaving the European Union, but it took four more years to actually do so. In the United States of America, an entrepreneur with no political experience became the forty-fifth president in January 2017. In October of the same year, the MeToo movement against sexual abuse and harassment started, with countless public allegations of sex crimes, as well as assessments of inequality. Following continuous police brutality, often resulting in death, against Afro-Americans in the United States, an international movement emerged against all forms of violence against black people. Information technology and smartphones play an important role in these evolutions: since 2010, the world has become an internet of both objects and subjects, continuously connected and updated by means of e-mail, Snapchat, Facebook, WhatsApp, Instagram, and Twitter. And finally, to end this decade—or to usher in the new one—a submicroscopic infectious agent replicating inside the cells of living organisms caused a tenacious pandemic, resulting in several million deaths and another abrupt end to many things that nearly everybody took for granted.

At first sight, none of this has anything to do with the Rolex Learning Center, the piece of architecture in Lausanne conceived by the Japanese architectural office SANAA. And what's more, despite everything that has happened since it's been put into use, the Rolex Learning Center has hardly changed. Day after day, it has continued to stand there, like buildings do—gloriously indifferent, or even scandalously disinterested—on the southern edge of the campus of EPFL, with Lake Geneva nearby, quiet and calm, and Mont Blanc crowning the view (surrounded most of the time by an immense expanse of blue sky, now and then scarred by an airplane). It is clear that the global

10

practice of architecture has changed since 2010, and that what is expected from buildings (and from architects as well as from architectural writers) has taken a few sharp turns, under the influence of historical developments. It would be extreme, but it is possible to consider the very notion of a building obsolete. Do we still have the luxury, from an ecological, social, political, and cultural point of view, to focus on buildings, instead of on environments, ecologies, people, power, inequality, and identity? Talking or thinking about the Rolex Learning Center today and looking back on its genesis and characteristics inevitably reflects those questions and changes, as they have been consequential for nearly everybody's vision of the world. It might even be possible to see many of these recent evolutions announced (well beforehand) by this building, or at least to retrace them retroactively in the building's characteristics.

And yet, despite everything, despite all that has changed, a work of architecture also has a lifespan—and installs a chronology—of its own. The Rolex Learning Center is a building of its time, of our time, but equally of that much different kind of time, a time that aspires to human universality, that is more immune to tidal waves of news items and current affairs, because it presents unchanging (or at least slowly mutating) conditions which stubbornly assert themselves over and over again. The time of a building, in other words, is also a kind of time that has to do with boring and basic (but never truly or definitely defined) activities, such as walking, talking, meeting, seeing, thinking, listening, learning, eating, reading, and living.

As with any building, the history and life of the Rolex Learning Center start long before its opening. Until the end of the 1960s, the campus it is now a part of didn't exist: agricultural crops such as corn and grain were cultivated there. On January 1st, 1969, the École Polytechnique Fédérale de Lausanne was founded according to the new Swiss Law on Federal Institutes of Technology. From that day onwards, the activities of the École Spéciale de Lausanne, which had been taking place in the city since 1853, started moving towards a vast area of farmland called Écublens, south of Lausanne and next to Dorigny,

where the University of Lausanne had begun installing itself. The open and relatively flat area of Écublens and Dorigny had been preserved as a whole throughout the twentieth century, and was destined to different but equally voluminous programs, such as an Olympic city, a military airport, and—after World War II, and with the Swiss national exposition of 1964 in mind—an airport for tourists travelling to Lausanne. None of these plans materialized, but all the while, surrounded by more and more houses, infrastructures, and roads, the void remained, seemingly waiting for all those students to arrive.

The relocation of universities, academies and schools out of cities to campuses in the former countryside became a nearly global phenomenon in the 1960s. Other activities and building types started to leave the city too, such as factories, hospitals, concert halls, or warehouses. For universities, the main reasons to move were simple: a dramatic increase in the student population, worn-out and scattered historical buildings, and not enough room for expansion in the city. What also played a part was that students had become increasingly articulate and politically conscious, most famously resulting in the revolts of May 1968. Whether the decision to transport these potential troublemakers was prompted by these uprisings, or whether the movement itself was a reaction to the relocation, is not easy to say. There is an anecdote about the French philosopher Henri Lefebvre, who was a professor at Nanterre University, which was built in the 1960s on the outskirts of Paris and which was the birthplace of the events of '68. When he was asked to explain why these revolts started in Nanterre, Lefebvre invited the interviewer to have a look at the campus from the window of his office. Who would not revolt if you had to study in such a terrible environment?

Something of these questions and debates is reflected—and refracted—by the complicated and contradictory situation in Lausanne. The democratization and expanded accessibility of higher learning which started in the 1950s did increase the student numbers and necessitate a move, but leaving the city did not meet with wholehearted approval. The students wanted to stay connected to city life, and the inhabitants of the immediate surroundings of Écublens and Dorigny were a bit afraid of the arrival of all those young people. It was therefore decided to turn the new accommodations of EPFL and UNIL not into fully-fledged campuses after the Anglo-Saxon model: students would not live on campus, and housing was not provided—a situation that has only quite recently, and in small measure, started to change.

It is always painful to disturb or destroy an immemorial and familiar landscape with architecture. This may be even more true in Switzerland than elsewhere. In his 1855 novel *Der grüne Heinrich*, Gottfried Keller allows one of his characters to say so clearly. "For the Swiss people especially, it would be folly to plaster their mountains with fine buildings; at the most perhaps a few fine-looking towns might be tolerated at the approach of them, but otherwise we must leave it to Nature to do the honors; this is not only the cheapest, but also the most judicious course." While it is clear that such an attitude is difficult to maintain in a modernizing country that doesn't want to condemn itself to economic decline, it is true that architecture in Switzerland has never really risen—if such a thing were possible—to the formal and scenic challenges offered by the scenery of the Alps. Topography and geography partly define national customs and ideology; mountains do induce a certain kind of piety, if only because they manifest the relativity of human undertakings, in terms of scale, lifespan, and coherence.

This can at least partly explain the architectural development of the EPFL campus. The design selected in 1970 following a national competition was a kind of technological system—a perpendicular grid of buildings and footpaths, supposedly rational while in reality often surprisingly labyrinthine, imposing a set of rules that could regulate not only people's behavior on campus, but likewise every possible expansion. While the project was indeed modest in terms of height, fragmentation, and durability (with self-cleaning aluminum facades, natural ventilation, and pedestrian mobility), it was rather overconfident in trying to capture both the use and the future of the campus. Additions and expansions in the following decades could understandably no longer stick to the formal language of the late 1960s, while variations on—rather than obedient extensions of—the existing structure seemed designated to increase, or at least to alter, the readability of the campus. The result, by the turn of the century, resembled a suburban office park, twice the size of the original megastructure of the 1970s, and almost completely devoid of free space, apart from a wide green lawn on the southern edge, separated from Lake Geneva by an interstate road and a handful of scattered private houses.

Great expectations and architecture often go together (and why shouldn't they?) but the future Learning Center had to meet many, many requirements; if every plot of land is an empty page waiting to be written upon, this one was more like a desktop upon which piles of papers and files were deposited. When the international architecture competition was launched in 2004, the new building was expected to contain many different and often competing activities: it needed to represent the library of the future, but it would also need to contain a multimedia collection, conference space, offices, meeting rooms, and places to study and rest, as well as a bookshop, a bank, and a restaurant. Apart from these functional requirements, and an accessibility all days of the week from early morning till late in the evening, the competition aimed to create the new heart of the EPFL—the only place on campus every student or professor would know and would make use of, possibly not every day, but at least on a regular basis.

The more difficult requirements were, as usual, symbolic and almost psychological: inside the building, all the different disciplines and knowledge areas of the academic community of EPFL would not only be able to meet but also to collaborate and exchange—to lift each other up to unprecedented heights of interdisciplinarity, simply by means of their new and very close proximity. And to top it all off, the future Rolex Learning Center was to become a symbol—something that everybody in the world outside would be able to identify with EPFL. In short, what the jury was looking for was an Eiffel Tower, a Piazza San Marco, a Crystal Palace, and a Web of Science, all at the same time.

A possibly unexpected but major challenge for all of the teams participating in the competition was the existing campus. Ten of the twelve projects consisted of an iconic, remarkable, and big building that tried to overpower the campus—in many cases by being visible, indeed like an Eiffel Tower, and by inviting everyone's attention, both up close and from far away. The beginning of the twenty-first century was still marked by heated architectural debates about self-important landmarks: spectacular buildings that tried to be different from their surroundings, but also, in many cases, different from what architects had produced and invented before. In a way, the competition at EPFL in 2004 coincided with the peak of this international discussion. (Not coincidentally, British architectural theorist Charles Jencks, known since the 1970s for capturing trends that were already on the verge of exhaustion, published his book *The Iconic Building. The Power of Enigma* in 2005.) Because the campus seemed to beg to be dominated—or retroactively structured, provided with a central point, and in a sense also completed—it seemed advisable to act accordingly. The formal and conceptual variety of answers provided by the invited architects is striking, and can serve as a far-reaching anthology of contemporary architectural strategies of the time: jewel-like, precious, and shiny objects (Zaha Hadid and Mecanoo); the huge blades of scissors, one directed towards the north, one to the south (Diller Scofidio + Renfro); an enormous viewing platform as an extension of the existing esplanade (Herzog & de Meuron); one long wall and an archaic structure in dark red concrete (Valerio Olgiati); a triangular bridge connecting the north and south parts of the campus (OMA / Rem Koolhaas); a massive disk of two floors, with zenithal light (Livio and Eloisa Vacchini); an angular, seemingly expandable modular tower building (Abalos & Herreros); a pyramid turned upside down and positioned in the middle of the esplanade (Xaveer De Geyter); and an anonymous cubic office building (Du Besset and Lyon). Alongside these ten entries, two others presented something quite different: their projects respected the sprawling character of the campus and acquiesced to the role of an addition instead of attempting to be a crowning achievement. This was possible either by adding several small buildings as pavilions that are part of an existing village-like settlement (what Jean Nouvel suggested), or by concentrating all the programmatic requirements in one big building, remarkably enough with only one undulating floor (what SANAA did).

The word *Sanaa* is of Arabic origin; it is a name for girls that means 'brilliance, brightness, radiance.' *Sanaa* (also spelled *Sana'a* or *Sana*) is the capital of Yemen, one of the oldest continuously inhabited cities in the world, with an inner core composed of many multi-story geometrically decorated buildings. SANAA, written in capitals, is an acronym that stands for Sejima And Nishizawa And Associates, a Tokyo architectural office established in 1995 by Kazuyo Sejima (1956) and Ryue Nishizawa (1966). During the 1980s, Sejima worked at the office of another Japanese architect, Toyo Ito (1941). In 1987, she established her own firm, where Nishizawa soon started working as a collaborator. Both partners of SANAA continue to develop individual projects and have worked together on a regular basis since 1995.

"Sejima is the bravest person I have ever known," Nishizawa has said in an interview. "Anyone who wants to design with her has to be daring. She is also very realistic, not a dreamer. She is very stable. I sometimes lose my way, when I suffer doing something. She never loses it." "In the beginning of the design process," Sejima added, "we tend to discuss a lot, not only with each other, but also with our staff. Gradually we move to the next phase through these conversations. I generally start to think in a direct way and Nishizawa tries to be more emotional. I think that he is more poetic than me." When Sejima was awarded the Erna Hamburger Prize for Woman Scientist of the Year in 2009, she talked about the advantage of collaboration: "To have an associate gives you support during those moments in life when you feel less productive, and vice versa."

To try to grasp what Sejima and Nishizawa have done in Lausanne, it is best to start with fundamentals: location, hierarchy, and centrality. A center can be defined in two ways that are not mutually exclusive. It is either the point equally distant from every point on the circumference of a circle (or on the boundaries or perimeter walls of a city), or it is the point from which an activity or process is directed, or on which it is focused.

According to the first definition, it is clear that the Rolex Learning Center is not centrally located. A collaborator of the Center for Biomedical Imaging has to walk at most two minutes to reach the main entrance, while walking from an office on the fourth floor of the architecture department can take up to seven minutes. Likewise, the second definition of the word "center" does not completely tally with the concept as it was defined prior to the competition: neither EPFL's activities nor its seats of power (the office of the president, for example) are concentrated within this building, and only some of the surrounding activities converge or meet their final destination inside. A crucial characteristic of the project proposed by SANAA in 2010 is that it seems to ignore this double fact—that the Rolex Learning Center is, in two ways, an *eccentric center*. Although it is located on the southern edge of the campus, it is designed to be equally accessible and open from all sides. Because of the expanse of space underneath the building, and because of the sloping floors, it is indeed possible to reach the entrance—and to "enter" the rectangle that is defined by this building—from any direction. And of course, the reverse is equally true: people can exit the Rolex Learning Center, more or less, just like rays that leave the sun, in all directions.

SANAA has therefore combined both a response to the need for a center (as a public meeting place for the campus and, ideally, for everyone else) and a total questioning of the main characteristics of a center. In the end, the very notion of a center (and the desire for it) no longer exists, if it has ever existed at all. This might well be one of the main characteristics of Japanese architecture—and of Japanese culture in general, including gastronomy, as it can be experienced and understood through Western eyes. In his 1970 book on Japan, *L'Empire des signes*, French author Roland Barthes suggested that "no Japanese dish is endowed with a *center* (the alimentary center implied in the West by the rite which consists of arranging the meal, of surrounding or covering the article of food). ... [O]n the table, on the tray, food is never anything but a collection of fragments, none of which appears privileged by an order of ingestion; to eat is not to respect a menu (an itinerary of dishes), but to select, with a light touch of the chopsticks." Applied to the Rolex Learning Center and the EPFL, SANAA's building not only respects the nature of the campus, but becomes, also in itself and in relation to its surroundings, "decentered, like an uninterrupted text," to borrow from Barthes' description of *sukiyaki*, a Japanese one-pot dish.

It is also unusual for a center to be empty. Of course, the Rolex Learning Center is not literally empty, like a desert, an unused notebook, or a USB-stick without data. In fact, because it is used so intensively, also by students from UNIL and by other visitors, it is often difficult to find free space. But at least theoretically, the center is *vacant*, certainly in comparison with all the other buildings on campus, which are explicitly predetermined to be used by a particular faculty or research group or by other members of the EPFL community. Compared to all those spaces and facilities, the hundreds of chairs and tables on the wavy floor of the Rolex Learning Center are undefined: no one has more right to claim them than anyone else. This turns the continuous interior into a different kind of working space—different, because the fixed activities and the defined roles people play on campus no longer seem to apply, at least not completely. Students are no longer part of an anonymous collective that needs to listen, in a group, to what their teachers are saying, and the academic staff is no longer confined to offices, laboratories, auditoria, or meeting rooms.

This does not mean, of course, that people come to the Rolex Learning Center to do nothing at all. But it does imply—or even impose—a different kind of activity once inside, as if all the other tasks and assignments are not allowed to enter and have to be left outside. Surrounded by a campus full of productivity and business, the Rolex Learning Center installs its own kind of occupation and concentration—an empty one, unscripted, not prescribed, as a kind of exception, or a possibility that is always there, when needed, as a breakout room or (why not?) a panic room. This is a phenomenon that Roland Barthes has also written about in his book on Japan. As any subway map of Tokyo shows, the enormously intricate network of metro lines—and all the activities and the traffic—circle around a center where The Imperial Palace is located. About that city center, Barthes wrote that it is indeed empty, "no more than an evaporated notion, subsisting here, not in order to irradiate power, but to give to the entire urban movement the support of its central emptiness."

Viewed in this way, the real function of the Rolex Learning Center lies not in what is happening inside, but rather in how it supports everything that happens elsewhere, simply by existing as a destination.

But aren't a lot of these characteristics applicable to every library, on every campus in the world? Differently put: wouldn't almost any design that had won the competition in 2004 have turned out to be a decentered center? Perhaps, but there is an important difference: the emptiness of SANAA's buildings, receptive of new events, activities, or interpretations, is an intentional part of SANAA's approach. Many critics and commentators have reflected on different aspects of what might amount to the same thing, namely elegance, pristineness, simplicity, lightness, clarity, thinness, subtlety, minimalism, or openness—characteristics applied so often to this oeuvre that they have become commonplace and possibly meaningless.

White is one of those words whose meaning remains uncertain. As a color, it has—to say the least—a tarnished history, and also in architecture, it has been mostly discussed in terms of suppression of everything and everyone that's *not* white. With Sejima's and Nishizawa's predilection for this color, something else is at stake. Its presence is most visible—and very aesthetically so—in the pictures taken of their buildings by Italian photographer Walter Niedermayr, who became known for his literally dazzling photographs of mountain landscapes, covered with thick layers of snow, sprinkled with at least a few small, candy-colored skiers or walkers, not unlike the staffage in Piranesi's etchings or in French landscape painting. It is unsurprising that Niedermayr and SANAA's paths would cross, and he has taken photographs of many of the Japanese duo's buildings.

The images Niedermayr took of the Rolex Learning Center are personal interpretations rather than truly realistic renderings. What distinguishes them from other photographs of the same building is indeed their quiet but slightly overexposed character, revealing a whiteness that might not literally exist in reality, but which is certainly part of the experience a building by SANAA can—or is intended to—offer. This white light homogenizes and attenuates the architecture, to such a degree that it becomes a natural presence, indeed not unlike a snow-white mountainside. The space becomes a kind of blank—an appearance of white that, rather than suppressing everything that exists, tries to form a neutral emptiness without meaning or symbolization on which skiers and students—or other forms of life—can mill about in all their complexity and unpredictability.

It is, again, something that Roland Barthes recognized when travelling to Japan, and when describing the Buddhist term *satori* as "a panic suspension of language, the blank which erases in us the reign of the Codes, the breach of that internal recitation which constitutes our person ... the *abolition* of secondary thoughts which breaks the vicious infinity of language." It is this kind of white emptiness that SANAA's architecture offers too—a void that exists for a few moments, and then gets broken and completed at the same time, just like in the photos of Niedermayr, by the presence of people.

All these qualities can indeed be considered Japanese, but this does not detract from the fact that the Rolex Learning Center is also a Western building, a creation that can easily be inscribed in the history of Western architecture. Japanese architecture has incorporated modernist and occidental influences with apparent ease, and traditional elements have merged with newer ones, although some of them have simply disappeared forever—something Jun'ichiro Tanizaki already warned of in 1933, in his famous book *In Praise of Shadows*. Rather than interpreting this influenceability as positive or negative, it suffices to understand this flexibility and openness (which also works in the opposite direction, since Western architecture has learned a lot from Japan) simply as one of its main characteristics. Architects, historians, and critics have been attracted by this paradox for decades: what is truly Japanese about architecture from Japan is that it has succeeded in being more relentlessly modern and Western than Western architecture itself.

In fact, all the aforementioned intellectual and all-too-human categories are often calmly but resolutely put aside by Japanese architecture, and distinctions like occidental and oriental, old and new, nature and culture, or modern and traditional, no longer apply. The well-known Hegel scholar Alexandre Kojève even went so far as to suggest that Japan is the only country in the world in which history has truly ended, simply because for several centuries no real political or economic changes and revolutions have taken place. The result is that things, and thus also buildings, can no longer be "dated": historical time and the possibility of change no longer exist, and the final consequence is a society in which everything is "formalized," in which content disappears, and meaning vanishes (something that Barthes also ascertained). Japan, Kojève suggested, does not have to fear becoming too Western—the opposite will take place: a "Japanization" of the Western world.

Kojève wrote this in the 1950s, and it is indeed a process that has been going on for quite a while. It can explain why it is not so hard to find antecedents for the Rolex Learning Center within the recent history of Western architecture. The most obvious predecessor of SANAA, among the generation of modernists from the first half of the twentieth century, is Mies van der Rohe. Not only do Sejima and Nishizawa share Mies's reluctance to speak, to interpret, and to comment upon their own designs, in their buildings they use, just like him, combinations of steel and glass to create impressions of transparency, invisibility, and flimsiness. It is with reason, therefore, that they have often been suspected of trying to "out-Mies Mies."

In 2008, Sejima and Nishizawa were invited to "do" something in the Barcelona Pavilion, designed by Mies and Lilly Reich in 1929, and reconstructed in 1986. "We decided," they wrote in a short, laconic explanation, "to use acrylic to make transparent curtains. We imagined an installation that leaves the existing space of the Barcelona Pavilion undisturbed." The curtain was shaped in a spiral, located in the interior of the pavilion, and it was almost invisible. Its effect proved nearly impossible to photograph, but the experience of the pavilion changed completely, as if it had become the decor of a hazy, druggy dream. That transparency always implies opacity—the hidden or even suppressed moral of Mies's oeuvre—was confirmed and made explicit by the presence of the polymer curtain inside this environment of glass.

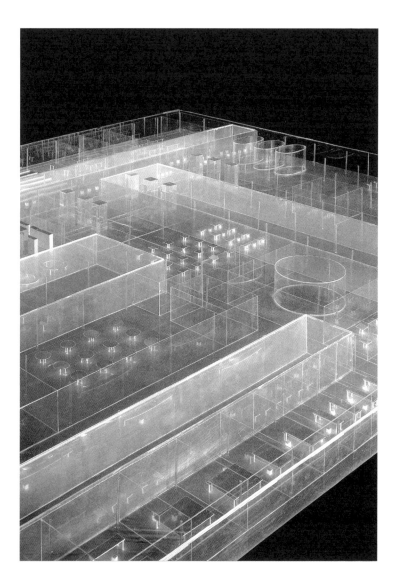

Earlier still, in 1997, SANAA participated in the competition for a new center for the Illinois Institute of Technology in Chicago, on a campus with a masterplan designed by Mies in 1939, in which he himself would complete no less than twenty-two buildings. SANAA proposed a reflecting, crystalline, glass box of only one floor—an extremely thin plate that again radicalized and literally outshone many of Mies's ideas, but that also can be seen as an early version, right-angled and fragile, of the Rolex Learning Center.

In Chicago, near the end of his life, Mies designed an office tower for the American multinational IBM, whose British headquarters across the Atlantic were designed in 1970 by Norman Foster. The latter building is another piece of architecture from the twentieth century that shows striking similarities to the Rolex Learning Center: it has almost the same length (but it is less deep), consists of a single floor clad in glass and steel, and is conceived as a succession of different working zones. SANAA's architecture, however, can in no way be categorized as high-tech, like the work of Foster and many of his British contemporaries, who tended to display—and at times fetishize—ducts, shafts, installations, elevators, and cables. An important part of Foster's building for IBM illustrates this: the technical ceiling, clearly visible from outside, like a separate story or an unemphatic corniche. In the work of Sejima and Nishizawa, technology continues to play an important part, but it has become less visible and more chimeric—it has evaporated, just like the technologies of wireless networks and data clouds that have become so defining for life in the twenty-first century.

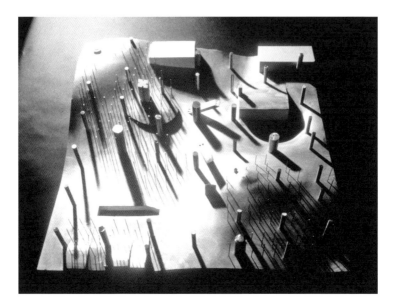

And of course, Foster's IBM building, as the epitome of rectangularity, doesn't wave. To find an undulating and more complex version of the same design, it is necessary to leap forward twenty more years, to the unexecuted 1990 design by OMA / Rem Koolhaas for a convention center in Agadir: a building resembling a hilly landscape, mimicking sand dunes, and structured by means of a forest of pillars. Again, the similarities with the Rolex Learning Center cannot be denied. But there are major differences too. What changed is that the roof in Lausanne no longer needs the support of pillars, as the floor only incidentally touches the earth, opening up a space underneath. The floor height doesn't change; both floor and ceiling remain parallel to each other, like two layers jumping up and down in a space without gravity. In this way, SANAA's project also revealed—and both strengthened and softened—the somewhat troubled or detached relationship with the earth's surface on EPFL's campus: many existing buildings don't have a real ground floor, and the lowest level is often actually below ground.

The structure of a building is never emphasized in SANAA's work, and the Rolex Learning Center forms no exception. The division of labor between the architect and the engineer—or between architecture and building—as it exists more or less since the beginning of the Renaissance, is not a gap they wish to bridge. Even more so: structural elements do not interest Sejima and Nishizawa, and the idea that architecture is first and foremost a matter of fighting gravity (and of honestly, proudly, and beautifully showing every step and strike of that fight) is foreign to them. Emphasizing visibility and counting on the display of materials and forces in order to establish truth—one of the main ambitions of modern architecture—has become somewhat of a lie in itself, or at least an illusion: we all know by now that what really matters—what is really *real*—is what remains invisible, beneath the surface, hidden from sight. From SANAA's point of view, architecture is therefore not a boxing match in which muscles and joints are primordial. It is a kind of ballet, a dance not unlike a painting by Matisse, in which bodies perform what they do not seem to be capable of and reach out their hands to form an equilibrium with each other, to draw a continuous line that divides or rather creates spaces, just by stretching and touching. The main tool Sejima and Nishizawa use during the design process (and photographs of their seemingly overflowing office in Tokyo testify to this) is the model, made out of cardboard, paper, or foam, that enables them to make space visible—thanks to but also despite the material that surrounds that space.

That is what also happened, more or less, with the Rolex Learning Center. SANAA and their collaborators made hundreds and hundreds of very different models—conceptual in nature, and of course not fully elaborated, showing almost every occupation imaginable of the available space, and accommodating the required functions. They selected the best option, refined it, won the competition, and then took the final model to the structural engineers, along with the question of whether it would be possible to build (although consultations with Mutsuro Sasaki, the engineer with whom Japanese architects such as Toyo Ito and Arata Isozaki have also collaborated, had of course taken place during the design process). This question was a major concern for the jury of the competition, and one of the members avowedly told Sejima that if the design were a student project at a school of engineering like the EPFL, it would not get a very high grade. The apparent irreconcilability of architecture and engineering—architecture comes first, and then the engineers march in—can be considered as something undesirable and even painful, certainly when taking into account the importance at EPFL of collaboration and interdisciplinarity. But it is also possible that the opposite is true: it is exactly because structural engineering is not SANAA's main concern that their proposals and designs pose an enormous and valuable challenge to structural engineers—it creates problems that would never have occurred to them if those crazy and presumptuous architects had not acted like what they are: crazy and presumptuous architects.

This is an issue that is more fundamental than it appears; it has to do with power, with otherness, with politics, and autonomy. It is perfectly feasible, in a manner of speaking, to lock up everyone involved in a certain project in one and the same oversized air-conditioned meeting room and to oblige them to come forward with a solution everybody agrees upon. But in that case, wouldn't the result inevitably be a compromise, or worse still, something imposed on all of the others by the most dominant, numerous, or wealthy party? It is therefore also supposable that in a collaboration, conflicts are not avoided, and everyone is allowed to do what they do best and what they are used to doing, on their own terms and within their own time. It is, again, because the architects of SANAA—and, one could argue, architects in general – do not think like engineers, that what they do can have real meaning for engineering.

The same can be said about digital evolution and, to put it a bit old-fashionedly, the computer. SANAA's work (and this applies to the majority of architects, whether we like it or not) has not been explicitly altered by the so-called digital turns—the introduction in the 1990s of computer-aided design, and the more recent advance of artificial intelligence, enabling a seemingly more open-ended, variable, and participatory design process. Rather than embodying or exemplifying these evolutions and revolutions, the Rolex Learning Center—and, again, so-called traditional architecture in general—enables us to confront them, as a building, literally and figuratively composed of screens, to look through, and to understand what is going on. Sejima said so very clearly at the beginning of her career, in a statement of principles she has repeated many times since: "Information and technology have helped to isolate the really distinctive features of architecture. This is the kind of positive approach I'm trying to advance."

It took two years to reconcile the image presented by SANAA in 2004 with technical and economic reality—proof that the choice for this particular project was not an easy one, or that it was at least a choice entailing a large number of (at the time) unanswered questions. The biggest problem to solve in order to get the Rolex Learning Center built, was the construction of shells perforated with patios: concrete shells have been constructed since antiquity, but mostly as a roof and not as a floor. Also, other issues—concerning programmatic requirements, accessibility, natural ventilation, possible deformation of the structure, and avoidance of counter-curvatures—had to be addressed. The risk was not only for the EPFL, but also for Sejima and Nishizawa: in case their plan proved to be a mirage, a pipe dream, or a cloud castle (and some competition renderings did point in that direction), the school would in all likelihood have needed to say goodbye to some of its ambitions, and the architects would have become known as, well, incompetent and unreliable.

The main challenge can be summarized as follows. The building consists of not two but three layers: the flat ground level, which is also the concrete ceiling of the basement floor (with a parking garage, toilets, and a large storage space for books and magazines); the first layer, which is the floor of the actual building, but also the vaulted ceiling of the open-air space underneath; and at the top the second layer, the upper roof. The middle layer was particularly difficult to construct, simply because it had to stand on its own: it could not rest on the ground floor, because that needed to remain open, and it could not depend on the roof for stabilization, because then the actual interior of the Rolex Learning Center would be crowded with columns instead of with people. Also difficult were the fifteen patios: they were necessary to let daylight in and to ensure access to the building, but they punctured the floor, drastically reducing its strength.

The strategy adapted by structural engineers Bollinger and Grohmann had more to do with the building of bridges than with architecture proper: the undulating floor would be connected with (and "secured by") the flat ground floor, not by means of vertical (and highly visible) supports, but by means of arches and beams. The floor plate is therefore constructed out of two concrete shells—one with a span of almost forty meters, and a second, larger one, spanning nearly eighty-five meters—combined with a series of eleven arches "anchored" in the roof of the basement. For the second shell, it proved nevertheless necessary to insert three vertical load-bearing elements (an elevator core, a wall, and a thick column) to guarantee sufficient stability. And even then, it was necessary, by means of digital software, to analyze (and to anticipate) the future behavior of these shells, with a vertical deflection of no less than fifteen centimeters. All this, in the end, made it possible to build extremely flat concrete shell structures. In comparison, the construction of the roof by means of a steel-grid structure with crossing continuous beams in wood and steel, aligned secondary girders, and a nine-meter column grid was almost disappointingly—or relievingly—banal.

Most concrete buildings are permanent structures that rely heavily on temporary ones; in the case of the Rolex Learning Center, because every form of engineering needed to be nearly invisible in the end result, the amount of formwork increased inversely. To create a mold in which the concrete could be poured (a process, by the way, that took a full forty-eight hours, uninterrupted), scaffolding towers were built with wooden tables on top. A consulting practice led by Fabian Scheurer was appointed to oversee the fabrication of the more than 10 000 individual pieces, including 1 500 tables measuring 2.5 by 2.5 meters. None of these tables—convex, concave, or nearly flat—were identical, and by means of the accessible and quite cheap software Rhino, a parametric 3D-model was developed, that could immediately define the dimensions of every single element. A system was thus installed to turn a complex thing into a simple and straightforward process—if SANAA wants to make a new Rolex Learning Center, somewhere else and with a different form, they could start right away, because the software is still available.

Despite this significant amount of computational thinking, some stages of the process could not be digitalized, and relied instead on craftmanship and DIY improvisation. Every wooden table, for example, was numbered at the time it was being cut. But because the worker wrote down the number wherever it was easiest for him to reach, once at the building site, it was impossible to tell the correct orientation of each wooden element—to determine without uncertainty which corner was supposed to go where. It was decided, therefore, to let the milling machine chamfer one corner of each table with an angle, to have a consistent reference mark. And once the concrete had hardened, all of the tables, in cheap, utilitarian OSB wood, were removed (requiring another temporary support of the shells by fifty-six hydraulic jacks) and consequently shredded, resulting in a big heap, next to the future Rolex Learning Center.

All that raises a by now inevitable question: is the Rolex Learning Center a sustainable building? According to the regulations and legislations valid during the first decade of the twenty-first century, the answer is yes. In terms of energetic performance—defined by the amount of energy needed to heat or to cool the building, and to ensure a comfortable indoor climate—the Swiss Minergie label for energy use was obtained, thanks to the dominance of natural lightning, the thick insulation for the roof and floor, the increased thermal inertia of the building, the use of underfloor heating, the combinations of natural and mechanical ventilation, and the automatically controlled metal shutters.

Since the completion of the Rolex Learning Center, however, criteria have been tightened. Climate change has motivated architects to not only consider the energetic performance of their buildings following completion, but also the energy used during construction, and thus the amount of carbon emitted prior to the opening of a building. Architecture is, ultimately and in many ways, a "carbon form"—it not only produces carbon before, during, and after construction, it can also confirm and strengthen those ways of life that thrive on carbon emissions.

SANAA's architecture, which by now can be found more or less all over the world, has been criticized as an "exercise in global production." In the most recent edition, published in 2020, of his classic book *Modern Architecture. A Critical History*, Kenneth Frampton devotes only a few sentences to the work of Sejima and Nishizawa. About the pavilion for the Toledo Museum of Art in Ohio, built in 2006 (and also a single one-story volume penetrated by courtyards), he writes: "Story-height sheets of iron-free plate glass were rolled in Germany, shipped to China where they were laminated, tempered, cut and bent, then transported to the United States where, to add insult to injury, they now enclose the Toledo Glass Museum in a city which, prior to the deskilling of American industry, had been one of the primary centers for glass production in North America."

The Swiss contracting firm Losinger Marazzi, when constructing the Rolex Learning Center, worked almost exclusively with national or even cantonal subcontractors. But because no single element in the facade's surface of almost 5 000 square meters is identical, it proved necessary to enlist the help of a Spanish firm for the production of energy efficient curved double glazing, as well as that of a Chinese firm for fabricating flat glazing panels that fit exactly between floor and ceiling. And even if these panels had been produced in Lausanne or somewhere else nearby, it would be clear by now that the Rolex Learning Center is anything but designed for the careful use of resources—its intentions, aspirations and qualities are simply on different planes. Whether this means a building like this one, and possibly architecture as we have known it in general, must become a thing of the past, is one of the more difficult questions the future has in store, certainly so long as both petro-consumerism and the worldwide quest for economic growth haven't been abandoned.

Neue Zürcher Zeitung

NZZ – ZEITUNG FÜR DIE SCHWEIZ

Donnerstag, 18. Februar 2010 · Nr. 40 · 231. Jhg.   gegründet 1780   www.nzz.ch · Fr. 3.50 · € 2.60

Eine Bibliothek wie eine Hügellandschaft
Die ETH in Lausanne verfügt mit ihrer neuen Bibliothek über einen architektonischen Blickfang, der zahlreiche Bewunderer in die Westschweiz locken wird. Die beiden japanischen Trendarchitekten Kazuyo Sejima und Ryue Nishizawa haben das Rolex Learning Center als hügeligo Lanchchaft konzipiert, die sich in der Mitte zu einer grossen Höhle aufwölbt. Feuilleton, Seite 55

Griechenlands verlorene Ehre

Neuer Streik – wachsende Gefahr sozialer Unrast

Die von den EU-Finanzministern beschlossene Verschärfung des Defizitverfahrens gegen Griechenland stösst in Athen auf Kritik. Es wird befürchtet, dass die Forderung nach weiteren Sanierungsmassnahmen soziale Unruhen auslösen könnte.

C. Sr. · In den griechischen Medien haben die Beschlüsse der Finanz- und Wirtschaftsminister der EU vom Dienstag einiges Unmut ausgelöst. Beinsel hält die von Athen bereits beschlossenen rigorosen Massnahmen zur Sanierung des Haushaltsdefizits für nicht genügend. Von einer beispiellosen Erniedrigung und von der verlorenen Ehre Griechenlands ist angesichts der als Zwangsverwaltung empfundenen strengen Kontrollen die Rede.

Verbreitetes Misstrauen

Ministerpräsident Papandreou, der nach einem überwältigenden Wahlsieg im Oktober das Amt des Regierungschefs übernommen hat, sieht sich einer doppelten Herausforderung ausgesetzt. Er muss bei im Ausland als Folge der Fälschung von Wirtschaftsdaten weit verbreitetes Misstrauen gegenüber Grie-

chenland zerstreuen. Zugleich befürchtet er, dass die Ram auferlegte Rosskur zu sozialen Unruhen führen könnte. Am Mittwoch sind die Zollbeamten in einen dreitägigen Ausstand getreten, am Freitag folgt ein Streik der Textilbüter. Für den 24. Februar haben Gewerkschaften des Landes zu einem Generalstreik aufgerufen.

Untersuchungskommission

Am Dienstag kündigte der Regierungschef die Bildung einer parlamentarischen Kommission an. Sie soll untersuchen, wer für die Fälschung von Statistiken, die Übermittlung manipulierter Wirtschaftsdaten an die Europäische Union und damit für die verlorene Ehre Griechenlands verantwortlich ist. Dem Bürger soll gezeigt werden, dass die für solche Misstände Verantwortlichen, welche die Glaubwürdigkeit des Landes zutiefst erschüttert haben, zur Rechenschaft gezogen werden.

Eine solche Untersuchung könnte aber auch zu neuen Spannungen zwischen den regierenden Sozialisten und der oppositionellen konservativen Nea Dimokratia führen und die Kommission gefährden, der bei der Umsetzung der rigorosen Sparmassnahmen dringend notwendig ist. International, Seite 5

EU drängt Bern und Tripolis

Calmy-Rey trifft in Madrid den libyschen Aussenminister

sig. · Nach der von Libyen verhängten Einreisesperre für Angehörige von 25 Schengen-Staaten ist der Druck auf die Schweiz am Mittwoch weiter gestiegen. Italien und Frankreich schwebt offenbar vor, dass die Schweiz und Libyen einen Vergleich abschliessen, möglicherweise unter dem Patronat der EU. Deutschland, das von der Visa-Krise verminscht hatte, verhielt sich in den letzten Tagen auffällig still.

Das Thema ist am Donnerstag in Brüssel in der Schengen-Visum-Gruppe und nächste Woche im Ausschuss für die Innenministern traktandiert. Das Amendwend (EDA) in Bern bekräftigte am Mittwoch, die Schweiz werde an ihrer restriktiven Visumpolitik gegenüber Libyen festhalten. Schweiz, Seite 11

Fritz Zurbrügg folgt auf Peter Siegenthaler

Schlüsselstelle beim Bund besetzt

smb. · Der Bundesrat besetzt eine Schlüsselstelle mit einem erfahrenen Ökonomen: Fritz Zurbrügg, der in Bern und Washington bereits wichtige Funktionen ausübte, wird neuer Direktor der Eidgenössischen Finanzverwaltung. Der 50-Jährige tritt die Stelle im Sommer an. Schweiz, Seite 12

Abfahrts-Gold an Favoritin Vonn

Suter Fünfte – Gisin stürzt

sda. · Die Amerikanerin Lindsey Vonn hat den Favoriten-Druck standgehalten und in der Olympia-Abfahrt in Whistler überlegen gesiegt. Sport, Seite 23 und 24

Altlasten beschäftigen den Bundesrat

Finanzmarktstrategie der Schweiz

hus. · Die Debatte über den Umgang mit unversteuerten Auslandvermögen auf Schweizer Bankkonti kommt nächste Woche in den Bundesrat. Wirtschaft, Seite 33

Tunen – aber richtig

WETTER
Einige Aufhellungen
Die Schweiz liegt an der Ostflanke eines grossen Tiefdruckgebietes.
Seite 32

INTERNATIONAL
Zäher Kampf der Nato gegen die Taliban
Seite 3

SCHWEIZ
Bescheidenes Rüstungsprogramm
Seite 11

ZÜRICH UND REGION
Wer soll was bezahlen in der Zürcher Pflege?
Seite 15

MEINUNG & DEBATTE
Hegemanns Kunst des frohen Zitierens
Seite 21

SPORT
Bertarelli will Alinghi weiterbringen
Seite 29

FOKUS DER WIRTSCHAFT
Das Fed in einer verzwickten Lage
Seite 40

Sportresultate 28   TV/Radio 31   Bildung 30   Anlagefonds 49–54   Veranstaltungen 56–62   Kino 60   Fahrzeuge 62   Trauer 10, 14

At the end of March 2010, only a few weeks after the opening of the Rolex Learning Center, the winner of that year's Pritzker Prize was announced—a prize awarded annually since 1979 and considered as the Nobel Prize for architecture. SANAA won, the jury explained, "for architecture that is simultaneously delicate and powerful, precise and fluid, ingenious but not overly or overtly clever; for the creation of buildings that successfully interact with their contexts and the activities they contain, creating a sense of fullness and experiential richness; for a singular architectural language that springs from a collaborative process that is both unique and inspirational." Similar praise had already been expressed for Sejima and Nishizawa's most recent building that featured in 2010 on the cover of a roll call of newspapers and international magazines.

What was questioned was the linking of architecture, technology, and construction, and if and how the resulting building not only accommodated the activities of a school, but also symbolized or inspired its mission and its future. Could the actual implementation, six years later, of the initial concept for the Rolex Learning Center be considered a compromise? And if so, was it nevertheless a successful or even an exceptional one? The experience offered by the interior was made possible by the engineering, and it was at the same time barely hindered by technical devices for lighting or ventilation on the floor or the ceiling. Some critics argued, however, that the limits of what is technically feasible were exceeded: the sought-after spatial continuity was not always guaranteed, for example in the outdoor space underneath the undulating floor where additional—and visible—concrete support proved necessary.

The value of the building was, in other words (and in line with what the architects said in interviews and during presentations), predominantly described in phenomenological terms—as a sublime and previously unseen space, highly functional but also continuous and overwhelming, that invited or provoked natural and sinuous movements, defined by accelerations, decelerations and digressions. "As in a landscape," wrote the editor in chief of the Italian magazine *Domus*, "the measure is that of a splendid measurelessness."

A similar view was offered by a possibly unexpected medium: film. At the end of August 2010, the 12th Venice Architecture Biennale opened, with the main exhibition entitled *People Meet in Architecture* curated by Kazuyo Sejima. In the Corderie dell'Arsenale, among many other things, *If Buildings Could Talk* was shown, a movie twelve minutes long directed by famous German producer Wim Wenders and commissioned by Sejima. Shot in 3D with two light photo cameras, the film tries to show activities unfolding inside and around the Rolex Learning Center: students reading and talking, visitors walking around, academics consulting. Two small electrical cars arrive, and the architects have a short cameo, flashing by on Segways with smiles on their faces. In an interview from 2010, Wenders shared his "theory about places": "they have stories to tell. If you are in a place for a while and if you are able to listen, you will hear the place's story."

The most important linguistic element in the film is indeed the female voice-over that makes the Rolex

Learning Center talk, and that addresses users and visitors. What the building says mostly relates to the spatial experience it has to offer, emphasizing the effect of the 3D-technology, and hinting at its possibly healing aspects: "I've noticed that people are often very busy, but sometimes ... very tired. Your time is so ... irregular. Sometimes I wish I could just calm you down a bit. My little hills try to do that."

It is rather hard to claim that a building can be sedating or therapeutic, but SANAA's architecture does have a particularly conditioning effect at times, and it seems to evoke a certain kind of calm, subdued, and controlled behavior. In the Louvre Lens, for example, the French art museum that opened in 2012, visitors line up neatly in the large entrance hall without being encouraged or forced. A lot of this has to do with the large amount of space that is available, and with the institutional idea and regime of the museum itself, but the architecture too—lucent, light, and thin—helps in creating a muted and concentrated atmosphere. Likewise, in the Rolex Learning Center, moving around is something you do quietly, and silence seems to impose itself naturally, also thanks to the endless expanse of gray carpet on the floor. Again, one could argue that this is something libraries just *do*; and architecture can—of course—never unilaterally define what will or will not happen inside its interiors. Rather, a building creates a probability of events, and to a higher or lesser degree it turns its users or visitors into characters or performers. Architecture makes stories possible, but some of these stories fit a particular building better than others.

What it is that this building would like us to do? And what does it enable us to see? Another precursor for the Rolex Learning Center from the twentieth century can help to answer that question: the Johnson Wax Headquarters, designed by Frank Lloyd Wright and completed in 1939 (except for the Research Tower, which came a decade later). As an administrative building for a factory of household cleaning supplies and other consumer chemicals, it was intended as an aesthetically pleasing workplace that would promote a sense of intimacy without confinement, but that would also enhance efficiency and productivity. The most impressive space in the building is the so-called Great Workroom, in a sense the very first open office landscape, measuring more than 1000 m^2. There are no windows, but soft yellow light radiates from the ceiling; the roof is supported by a field of white dendriform columns, with such a slender base that building inspectors were at first very skeptical and asked for a test column to be built, after which the structure proved to remain intact. Wright wanted the office building and the workspaces to be "as inspiring to live and work in as any cathedral ever was to worship in."

Rather than a classical library in which to read, to study and to learn, the Rolex Learning Center is more akin to a kind of open office landscape—a *burolandschaft*, as the genre was coined in the 1950s in Germany—just like the Great Workroom of Frank Lloyd Wright. But the big difference is that it doesn't have a traditional flat floor surface, but a ground level with many slopes, hills, and valleys. The result is a continuously flowing space in which hard boundaries may be absent, but in which smaller divisions and more intimate zonings do nevertheless occur, albeit in ways that are difficult to fathom. In other words: what the building is withholding, inside, is an overview—a rational, all-encompassing, panoptical view, available at a glance, of what is happening and what is taking place.

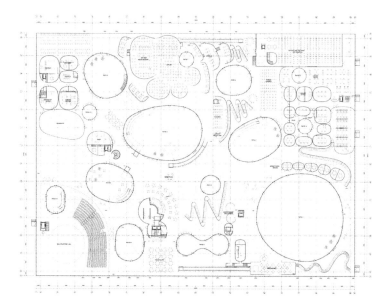

That is why, despite all its ostensible transparency, the Rolex Learning Center remains a slightly abstruse and opaque building, mainly because it does not divide things and people into clear-cut categories and spaces. Likewise, differences between studying or socializing, producing or consuming, eating or napping, writing, texting or reading, relaxing or stressing, watching or listening, are all difficult to sustain; in short, the distinction between work and life has been erased, and what opens up is a kind of total space for a total existence, that—depending on one's own poise and sensibility—can be devoid of everything or on the contrary filled to the brim. The building has been criticized for this, too—for creating the atmosphere of a beautiful lounge in which students and staff are nevertheless continuously advised to be silent, to work, and to be productive. Thinking back to the events of 1968, the subsequent and slightly paranoid question then seems to be: does this architecture encourage a kind of critical and autonomous thinking, or is rather the opposite true?

Looked at in more neutral terms, it is undeniable that the Rolex Learning Center does not gloss over or nostalgically conceal the way we live and work now. "I concede," Sejima has said in an interview early on in her career, "that I am indeed living within the present. But that is all the more reason why I don't believe in trying to deny or conceal that fact by creating oppositional architecture. Nor am I simply reiterating contemporary society in its current form. I actually think it is rather puzzling that an architect would premise his work on a fictional idea and then try to convince others that it is a reality. To use my architecture as a device that simply exposes the various social constraints would do little more than reify their presence. Instead, I look at architecture as a vehicle that enables us to get a better grasp of society or culture."

What this position means for the Rolex Learning Center can be understood by means of a metaphor. Swiss art and architecture historian Kurt W. Forster sharp-wittedly suggested that being inside SANAA's New Museum in New York, completed in 2007 as a collection of boxes stacked on top of each other, "might be compared to being inside a MacBook." It is highly likely that this metaphor applies even more to the Rolex Learning Center. This has not so much to do with the color white—a color Apple has left behind for more than a decade now—or with the presence of MacBooks on most of the tables inside of the Rolex Learning Center, if only because many other devices, running on other operating systems like Windows or Linux, are present in abundance too. The real similarity to the MacBook has to do with the mental atmosphere it offers, and with the theoretically endless flow of very diverse applications, connections, and activities it has in store—simultaneously and side by side. Of course, this is a state, one could argue, that is defined exactly by the fact that it is no longer linked to one specific location: making full use of a MacBook is possible wherever Wi-Fi is available. The Rolex Learning Center is, nevertheless, one of those few buildings in which that very contemporary (and placeless) state of being finds a true place of its own—a home, so to speak.

"A major work will either establish the genre or abolish it; and the perfect work will do both." This famous definition of perfection was written by German critic Walter Benjamin in 1928. When applying this criterium to the Rolex Learning Center, Benjamin could suggest that SANAA's building at the same time abolishes the genre of the library and that of the open office space, by gently and elegantly, but without wavering, convincing both to cohabitate between two undulating but continuously parallel layers.

That is why, after examining its precursors, it is nothing but appropriate to ascertain the architectonic progeny of this merger. Regarding SANAA's work since 2010, it is true that this building was kind of an endpoint for them—not because they have ceased their activities, but because both the formal and the programmatic experiments of the Rolex Learning Center have reached their apogee and have been succeeded by other explorations and investigations, dealing with multiple floors, for example, more irregular roofs, or direct and less orthogonal connections to the environment. Other contemporary architects have continued to develop projects or buildings that resemble landscapes—as so-called "megaforms" or "landforms"—but all in all the emphasis has shifted towards the smaller scale: the classical, recognizably urban form, or the building as a modest, temporary process, rather than as a labor-intensive and drastic enterprise of epic proportions.

Regarding spaces for working and learning, a two-part evolution is noticeable since 2010. On the one hand, the importance of the open office floor has been spectacularly confirmed—it continues to be the norm, without restraint, and with extreme consequences. In 2015, possibly the largest room in the world was built—an uncharacteristically modest design by Frank O. Gehry, accommodating the working space for Facebook employees in Menlo Park, California, and inducing flexibility, fast-paced brainstorm sessions, as well as the sheer inability to be alone. With a floor surface of approximately 40 000 m^2, it is almost twice the size of the Rolex Learning Center, but it is of course not a public building, and it is much more raw and unrefined.

On the other hand, the global pandemic that started in 2020 at times seems to have sufficiently proven the total relativity of space and architecture for work, production, and collaboration. Who needs an enormous open office floor when you have Zoom? Even when it has become clear how much we can do in our room, at home, all by ourselves behind a computer screen, one of the most important functions of architecture is still, as Rem Koolhaas predicted at the end of the previous century, "the creation of the symbolic spaces that accommodate the persistent desire for collectivity." The Rolex Learning Center is one of the more important recent monuments to that idea.

In the end, the value and legacy of what was completed by SANAA (and many others) in 2010 in Lausanne, does not lie in what the building created, or in how it has been imitated, criticized, praised, succeeded or copied. Its real importance lies in its continued daily functioning, as well as in the way it durably symbolizes EPFL, not so much as a logo, but more as a floating signifier, able to adapt and attract meanings depending on the occasion, the strategies, and the points of view.

The most lasting and perhaps surprising impression it can make has to do with knowledge and understanding. Some buildings are self-evident and (in a positive way) banal. Some buildings try to impress by wearing ideas and intelligence on their sleeves. Other buildings are remnants of convictions or beliefs that have since disappeared. And then there are buildings that, when looked at and examined from the right angle, release the knowledge they contain slowly, consistently, through the years, and only after concentrated insistence. These buildings, and the Rolex Learning Center is one of them, are places that can be, all by themselves, an almost inexhaustible source of higher knowledge.

Acknowledgements

The author would like to thank Cyril Veillon from Archizoom, Lucas Giossi from EPFL Press, and Bettina Caruso and Mirko Bischofberger from Mediacom for their support, André Patrão and Stéphanie Savio for their comments on an earlier version of this text, Janice Gaugenot for the proofreading, and Marie Lusa for her graphic design.

Bibliography

Three books have been devoted to the Rolex Learning Center and its history, all published by EPFL Press: Della Casa, Francesco and Patrick Aebischer, *Rolex Learning Center*, 2010; Francesco Della Casa, Jacques Perret, *Rolex Learning Center—English Guide*; Philip Jodidio, *Views Rolex Learning Center*, 2015. ● About the architectural competition for the Rolex Learning Center, see Robert Walker, "Futuristische Lernlandschaft," *Werk, Bauen + Wohnen* 92 (2005), 56–58. ● Many reviews were published before or after completion, such as Sony Devabhaktuni, "A Little Place Called Space," *AA Files* 58 (2009), 74–77; Rob Gregory, "SANAA Creates a Blank Canvas," *Architectural Review* 1358 (2010), 22–23; Hannes Mayer, "Die Welt ein Kreis, die Welt eine Linie," *Archithese* 3 (2010), 80–85; Flavio Albanese, "A Solid Garden," *Domus* 934 (2010), 17–26; Angélique Vossnacke, "Schwingender Saum," *Baumeister* 4 (2010), 46–53; Francesco Buzzi and Tibor Joanelly, "Weisse Leere," *Werk, Bauen + Wohnen* 5 (2010), 10–19; Jacques Lucan, "No-Stop Building," *Casabella* 790 (2010), 6–10; Andreas Rumpfhuber, "The Legacy of Office Landscaping," *IDEA Journal* 1 (2011), 20–33. ● Construction and ventilation were the subject of *Tracés* 135 (2009), 5–27 and *Detail* 5 (2010), 470–481. See also Christian Maillet, "Les coques du Rolex Learning Center," in *L'architrave, le plancher, la plate-forme. Nouvelle Histoire de la construction*, ed. Roberto Gargiani, Lausanne, EPFL Press, 2012, 882–888. ● Interviews with Kazuyo Sejima and Ryue Nishizawa can be found in *El Croquis* 77 (1996),

99 (2000), 139 (2008), 155 (2011), 179 / 180 (2015), 205 (2020), as well as in Hans Ulrich Obrist, *SANAA. Kazuyo Sejima & Ryue Nishizawa. The Conversation Series 26*, Cologne, Walther König, 2012; *The SANAA Studios 2006–2008. Learning from Japan: Single Story Urbanism*, ed. Florian Idenburg, Baden, Lars Müller Publishers, 2010. • The Rolex Learning Center and the work of SANAA were the subject of the following book chapters: "Control Yourself! Lifestyle Curation in the Work of Sejima and Nishizawa," in *Architecture at the Edge of Everything Else*, eds. Marrikka Trotter and Esther Choi, Cambridge / London, MIT Press, 2010, 22–33; "Organize / Optimize / Simplify / Materialize. Fabian Scheurer interviewed by Marc McQuade" and "Engineering the EPFL Rolex Learning Center. Bollinger + Grohmann," in *Landform Building*, eds. Stan Allen and Marc McQuade, Baden, Lars Müller Publishers, 2011, 408–454; "Soft Manifesto," in Beatriz Colomina, *Manifesto Architecture*, Berlin, Sternberg Press, 2014, 29–38; Marc Frochaux, "The Environment of Knowledge," in *The Building*, ed. José Aragüez, Baden, Lars Müller Publishers, 2016, 286–295. • The anecdote about Henri Lefebvre in Nanterre is recounted in Lukasz Stanek, *Henri Lefebvre on Space: Architecture, Urban Research, and the Production of Theory*, Minneapolis, University of Minnesota Press, 2011, 186. • The book by Roland Barthes on Japan was translated into English by Richard Howard as *Empire of Signs*, New York, Hill and Wang, 1982. • The photographs of SANAA's buildings by Walter Niedermayr are the subject of Moritz Küng, *Kazuyo Sejima + Ryue Nishizawa / SANAA & Walter*

Niedermayr, Ostfildern, Hatje Cantz Verlag, 2007.
● Alexandre Kojève's remark on the end of history in Japan can be found in *Introduction to the Reading of Hegel. Lectures on the Phenomenology of Spirit*, Ithaca, Cornell University Press, 1980, 162. ● The notion of "carbon form" was coined and defined by Eliza Iturbe in *Log* 47 (2019). ● The Rolex Learning Center appears, as a subject or decor, in three movies: *If Buildings Could Talk* (2010) by Wim Wenders, *Le paysage intérieur* (2010) by Pierre Maillard, and *L'amour est un crime parfait* (2013) by Arnaud and Jean-Marie Larrieu. ● The interview with Wim Wenders by Anna Battista was published in 2010 in *Zoot Magazine* and is available online. ● The buildings for the Johnson Wax Headquarters are the subject of Jonathan Lipman, *Frank Lloyd Wright and the Johnson Wax Buildings*, New York, Rizzoli, 1986. ● The essay by Kurt W. Forster on SANAA's New Museum was published in *Log* 12 (2008), 5–12. ● The quote by Walter Benjamin can be found in *The Origin of German Tragic Drama*, London / New York, Verso, 1998, 44. ● For more on the Facebook Headquarters, see Georgios Eftaxiopoulos, "The Largest Room in the World. MPK20 and Hyper-Flexibility," *AA Files* 77 (2020), 89–112. ● The quote by Rem Koolhaas can be found in OMA / Rem Koolhaas & Bruce Mau, *S,M,L,XL*, Rotterdam, 010 Publishers, 1995, 604.

Captions

p. 8 Banner from Extinction Rebellion in Trafalgar Square, London, October 10, 2019, Wikimedia Commons. p. 10 Ferdinand Hodler, *Der Genfersee von Lausanne aus*, 1912, private collection, Wikimedia Commons. pp. 12–14 Jean-Michel Zellweger, *Vaud du ciel. Tome 1*, Lausanne, EPFL Press, 2018. p. 14 Student Manifestation in front of Lausanne Station, May 1968, ASL-Fotoagentur, Schweizerisches Nationalmuseum. p. 16 Écublens, Rue de Bassenges, Préverenges, 1940–1950, Musée Historique Lausanne. p. 18 Sebastian Vrancx, *A Carnival Scene at the Piazza San Marco*, 1605, private collection. p. 20 Madelon Vriesendorp, *Chess Game*, Rolex Learning Center EPFL, 2011. p. 22 Sanaa, Capital of Yemen, Wikipedia Commons. p. 20 Sushi Dinner, personal collection, 2019. pp. 28–29 Sofia Coppola, *Lost in Translation*, 2003, still, American Zoetrope. pp. 32–33 Walter Niedermayr, *Schnalstalgletscher 99/2018*, Diptych, Galerie Nordenhake Berlin / Stockholm, Ncontemporary Milano, Galerie Widauer Innsbruck, 2018. p. 36 Wim Wenders, *Tokyo-Ga*, 1983–85, still © Wim Wenders Stiftung, 2014. p. 40 SANAA, Intervention in the Mies Van der Rohe Pavilion, Barcelona, 2008. p. 38 SANAA, Competition Design for the IIT New Campus Center, Chicago, 1998. p. 44 Norman Foster & Partners, IBM Pilot Headquarters, Cosham, UK, 1971. p. 46 OMA / Rem Koolhaas, Agadir Convention Center, 1990. p. 48 Henri Matisse, *La Danse*, 1910, St. Petersburg, The Hermitage. p. 50 Merel Vos, Working Experience SANAA Tokyo, 2008. p. 52 Jérémie Souteyrat, Office of Ryue Nishizawa,

December 9, 2010. p. 54 Le Corbusier, *Open Oyster Shell*, 1932, Pencil, pastel, FLC 1967, Fondation Le Corbusier, Paris. p. 56 Alain Herzog, Construction Site Rolex Learning Center, Lausanne, January 31, 2007. p. 58 Fabian Scheurer, Concrete Formwork Tables Shredded After Use, Lausanne, 2007, Design-to-Production, Zürich. p. 60 Manifestation Jeunes Vert-e-s Suisse, February 4, 2019, Lausanne. p. 62 Assemblage of Glass Element for the Toledo Museum of Art Glass Pavilion, March 22, 2006, Paratus Group, New York. p. 64 Front Page of the *Neue Zürcher Zeitung*, February 18, 2010. p. 68 Wim Wenders, *If Buildings Could Talk*, 2010, still © Neue Road Movies, photograph by Donata Wenders, 2010. p. 70 Jack E. Boucher, The Great Workroom in The Johnson Wax Corporation Building by Frank Lloyd Wright, 1969 (1939), Library of Congress. p. 72 SANAA, Rolex Learning Center, Lausanne, 2010, Floor Plan. pp. 74–75 SANAA, New Museum, Corridor, New York, 2008, Nathan Willock VIEW. pp. 78–79 Frank O. Gehry, Facebook Campus Headquarters, MPK20, Menlo Park, California, 2012. p. 82 Alain Herzog, Entrance to the Forum of the Rolex Learning Center, Lausanne, 2012.

The image at the back cover is a still from *Le paysage intérieur* (2010) by Pierre Maillard, CAB Productions, Lausanne.

EPFL

The publisher and authors express their thanks to the École polytechnique fédérale de Lausanne (EPFL) and ARCHIZOOM for its generous support towards the edition of this book.

The EPFL PRESS is the English language imprint of the Foundation of the Presses polytechniques et universitaires romandes (PPUR). The PPUR publishes mainly works of teaching and research of the EPFL, of universities and other institutions of higher education.

ARCHIZOOM is the exhibition and lecture space of the ENAC School at EPFL.
www.archizoom.ch

Presses polytechniques et universitaires romandes
EPFL – Rolex Learning Center
Post office box 119
CH-1015 Lausanne, Switzerland
info@epflpress.org
Phone: +41 (0)21 693 2130

www.epflpress.org

© 2021, first edition, EPFL PRESS
ISBN 978-2-88915-422-7

Graphic Design: Studio Marie Lusa & Dominique Wyss

Printed in Switzerland